Wash, scrub, brush!

Written by Mick Manning
and
illustrated by Brita Granström

Albert Whitman & Company
Morton Grove, Illinois

Someone's having a party,
and we're all invited!
But first we have to be nice and clean.
We need to…

wash, scrub, brush!

Animals, birds—even insects
wash, scrub, and brush!

There are more harmful germs and bacteria under your fingernails than on a toilet seat!

Someone's got long, yucky nails—
they look like monster claws!
We've got to trim them and clean them
in time for the party…

Wash, scrub, brush!

A Komodo dragon's claws are so dirty that just a scratch from them can cause a nasty infection.

5

Someone's got very dirty ears!
And what's all this stuff behind them?
Wash them out gently
before you go to the party…

Wash, scrub, brush.

Ears are very delicate and we have to be gentle when we clean them. Rabbits clean their ears very carefully!

African oxpeckers eat the ear wax of zebras and other animals.

6

Someone's teeth are all icky with food,
and smell that doggy breath!
You'd better brush your teeth
before we phone a vet!

Wash, scrub, brush.

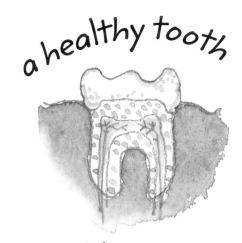

a healthy tooth

Plaque builds up on your teeth. When you eat sugar, the plaque turns to acid— that's how cavities happen!

This grouper fish is letting smaller fish clean his teeth— he gets clean teeth, they get a meal!

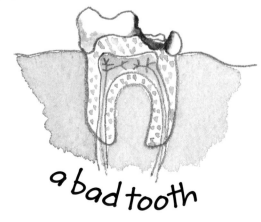

a bad tooth

Someone smells like they've laid
a rotten egg. Phew!
I'll change the baby's diaper
while you go straight to the bathroom!

Wash, scrub, brush.

We need toilet paper to wipe our bottoms!

Otters go to the bathroom
in special places to
mark out their territory.

10

We can clean up after ourselves, but babies need help. They have diapers that need to be changed often.

Someone needs to wash their hands
after going to the bathroom.
You don't want to spread germs—
or worms!

Wash, scrub, brush.

Kittens and puppies often have worms
when they are born. They need to be
wormed by a vet.

It's easy to pick up germs. That's why washing your hands is so important!

Pinworms are tiny, and they make your bottom itchy.

Pinworms ↑

13

Someone's been running around
getting all hot and sweaty!
You'll feel much better
after taking a shower…
Wash, scrub, brush.

Elephants have showers, too—they use their long trunks!

Someone looks like they've been
rolling around in the mud!
You need a bath,
and your clothes do, too!

Wash, scrub, brush.

Mud seems messy to us, but hippos and many other animals use mud to stay cool or clean away insects!

Someone's hair looks like
it needs a good brushing.
You can't go to the party
when your hair looks like a bush!

Wash, scrub, brush.

Even Arctic foxes like
a good scratch!

Birds brush or "preen" their feathers every
day to keep them in good condition,
using a special oil from a gland under
their tail.

19

Dandruff is caused by dry, flaky skin and by oily glands in your scalp.

Someone's hair looks dirty and dull.
Let's give it a sudsy shampoo.
Soon it'll be clean and shiny—
just right for the party!

Wash, scrub, brush.

A sloth's hair is full of moss and lichen! But it needs to be that way—staying "dirty" keeps sloths hidden from danger.

Ants help clean the feathers of some birds, like jays. The ants squirt out a sort of acid that kills bugs.

Someone's got lice! Oh, no!
It's not your fault—
Mom will carefully comb out the nits
and then use the special shampoo.

Wash, scrub, brush!

Monkeys groom each other's fur and eat the nits—very tasty!

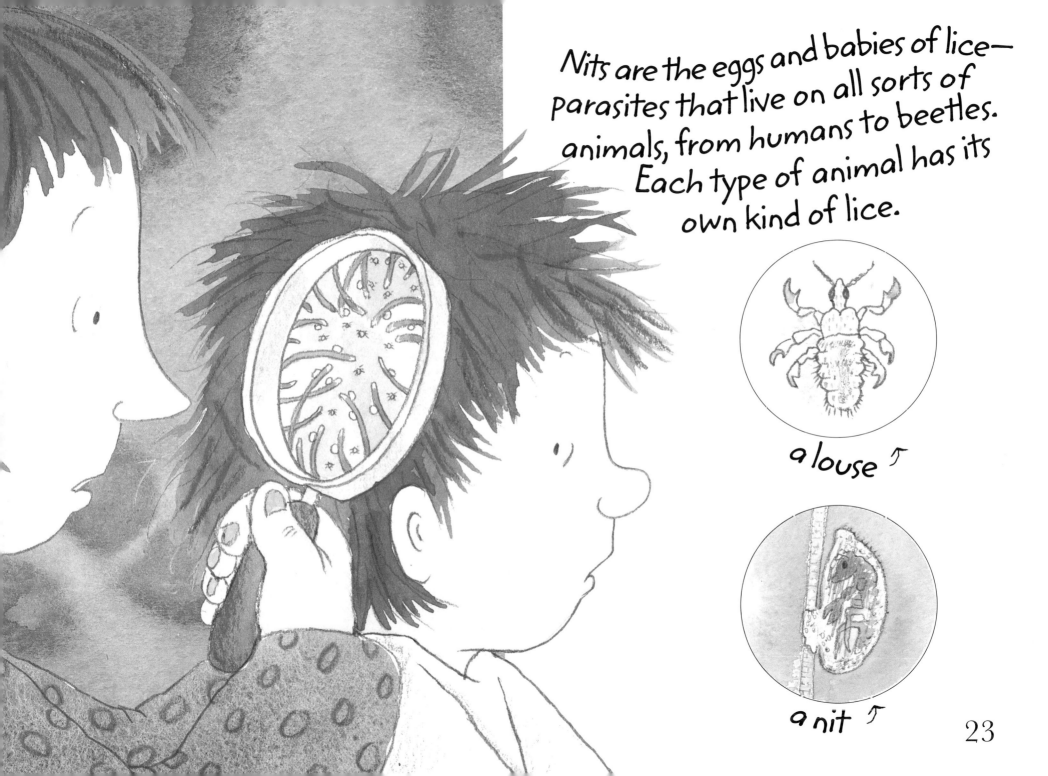

Nits are the eggs and babies of lice—parasites that live on all sorts of animals, from humans to beetles. Each type of animal has its own kind of lice.

a louse ↑

a nit ↑

23

We all need to stay clean and fresh. It just takes a little soap and water… Every day!

Welcome to our party!

Every day we need to…

26

Wash, scrub, brush!

27

Keeping Clean...

Feet
Clean feet and fresh socks help stop the bacteria that cause smelly feet!

Clothes
Clean clothes keep you fresh and feeling good!

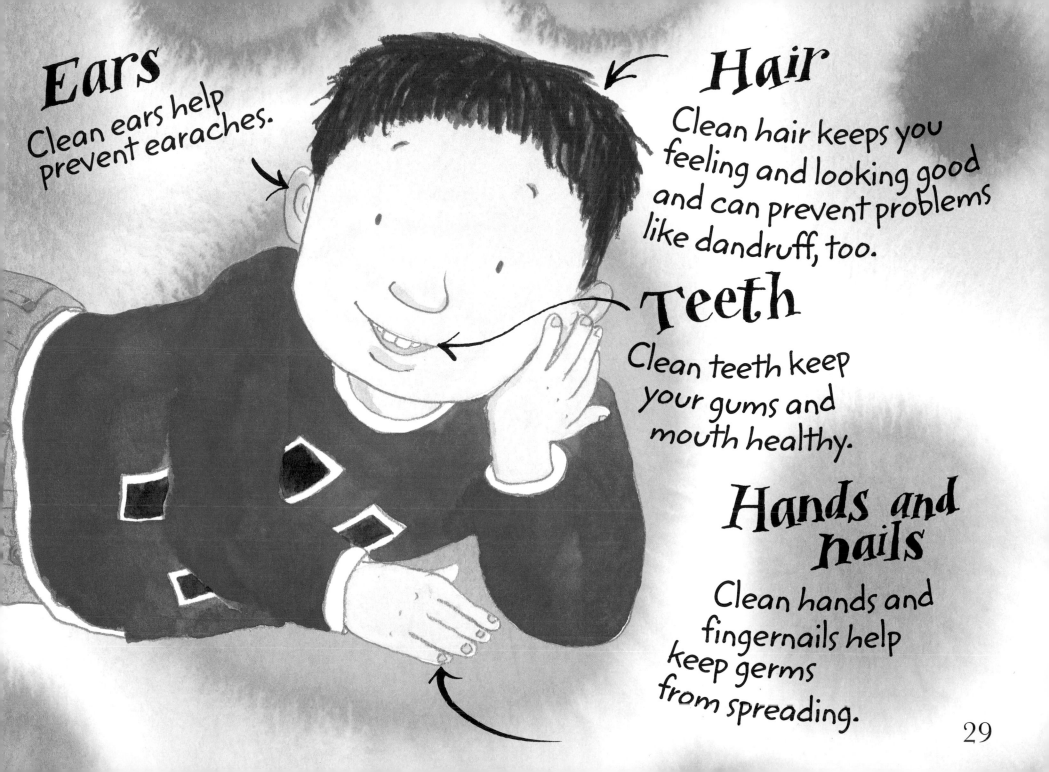

Ears
Clean ears help prevent earaches.

Hair
Clean hair keeps you feeling and looking good and can prevent problems like dandruff, too.

Teeth
Clean teeth keep your gums and mouth healthy.

Hands and nails
Clean hands and fingernails help keep germs from spreading.

29

Useful words

Bacteria live on and around us—they're part of the group of small living things called germs. Some kinds of bacteria don't bother us, but other kinds can cause infections (see pages 4, 5).

Ear wax is the yellow wax that builds up inside your ear holes. It protects your ears and helps you hear better. Other animals have ear wax, too (see pages 6, 7).

Germs are tiny plants and animals too small to see. They carry and spread diseases such as coughs and colds (see pages 4, 5, 12).

Glands are places in the bodies of humans and animals that produce sweat or oil (see pages 19, 20).

Infection is a sort of disease that is spread by germs or bacteria (see page 5).

30

Parasites are animals that live in or on another animal, feeding off it and laying their eggs on it. Lice are parasites; so are some kinds of worms (see pages 12, 13, 22, 23).

Pinworms are small white parasites. A person with pinworms gets an itchy bottom from the worms' eggs. If eggs get onto your hands they can spread to other people. It is easy to get rid of worms with some medicine (see pages 12, 13).

Plaque is a type of bacteria that grows on teeth and gums. When plaque mixes with sugar from food, it makes an acid that causes teeth to decay (see pages 8, 9).

Territory is the name given to the area a particular animal lives and hunts in. Some animals do not like to share their territory with other animals of the same type, so they mark their territory to tell others to stay off (see page 10).

For Mia, Jan-Erik, Albin, Gabriel and André
—M.M. and B.G.

First published in 1999 by Franklin Watts, 96 Leonard Street,
London EC2A 4XD.

Library of Congress Cataloging-in-Publication Data

Manning, Mick.
Wash, scrub, brush! / by Mick Manning;
illustrated by Brita Granström.
        p. cm.
        ISBN 0-8075-8668-4 (hbk.)
1. Baths—Health aspects–Juvenile literature. 2. Children–Health
and hygiene–Juvenile literature. [1. Cleanliness. 2. Grooming.
3. Animals–Grooming behavior.] I. Granström, Brita. II. Title.
        RA777 .M265 2001
        613'.4—dc21
        00-010518